Holocaust Forgotten - Five Million Non-Jewish Victims

By: Terese Pencak Schwartz

Even though this book was written, edited and published by the author, several stories were contributed by individuals who submitted manuscripts for inclusion.

Individual contributors include:
John Millrany
Grace de Ronde
Susan Ost-Perrone
Zygfryd P. Baginski
Joseph S. Wardzala
Michel Depierre and Peter Branton
Curtis M. Urness, Sr.
Ryan Bank

Image montage on back cover created by Felix Stohlmann
Photograph of Jan Karski - Courtesy of The Hoover Institution

Cover design by Christine Ticali - Dark Road Designs

To my beloved mother, Ewa Pencak, whose legacy I inherited, and to my dearly loved daughter, Sophia Eve Schwartz, who will become heir to it.

Table of Contents

Acknowledgements

In addition to the contributors who have allowed me to include their stories in this book, there have been many others whose efforts and encouragement made this work possible including: Prof. Dr. Zdzislaw P. Wesolowski, Rabbi Harold M. Schulweis, Edward Lucaire, Stefan Korbonski, Richard C. Lukas, Robert Strybel, and my mother, Ewa Pencak.

Foreword

Every semester, I ask my university students, "What was the first and last group of people the Nazis mass murdered?" They are confident of their reply. "The Jews," they say, without hesitation. Some, adopting an air that indicates that they imagine themselves privy to information others lack, report "Homosexuals," or "Communists." No one ever gets it correct. I ask others, as well, including the PhDs among my colleagues. They don't know, either. The first and last group that the Nazis murdered was handicapped people. When I tell my interlocutors this, they are shocked. They assume I am wrong. They promise me that they will Google this question. How could they be so misinformed about something so important?

It makes perfect sense for the Nazis to have mass murdered handicapped people first and last. That mass murder is entirely in line with Nazi ideology. The Nazis, as Richard Weikart demonstrated in "Hitler's Ethic: The Nazi Pursuit of Evolutionary Progress," founded their genocides on a consistent ethic. Their ethic was inspired by atheism, neo-Paganism, and Scientific Racism. Their ethic was voiced before Hitler ever rose to power, by the Scientific Racists in the U.S. who reacted with horror to new, undesirable, peasant immigrants from places like Poland and Italy.

We need to understand Nazism, and we will not do so until as many people who know the number "six million" also know the number "five million." We need to know that the five million were not killed "by accident" but very much in line with Nazi ideology. It is difficult to penetrate this thicket of hostility to the story of the Nazi victimization of non-Jews, but Terese Pencak Schwartz has done so, admirably. Terese Pencak Schwartz is a heroine in this battle for truth and understanding. Her success is to every one's benefit; without the kind of information that she insists on presenting, we cannot begin to understand what we do know of the Nazis, or of the Holocaust.

Danusha V. Goska, PhD

Chapter 1 - Five Million Forgotten

Raised by parents who had survived the Holocaust, I heard many stories about the atrocities of this World War II horror. I learned how one of my family's homes in Poland was burned to the ground by Nazis. I learned that my uncle was shot in the head by Nazi soldiers because his family was hiding a Jewish woman. Painful as it was for them to speak about it, my parents [Frank and Ewa Pencak] felt it was important that I knew the stories of the Holocaust.

It was only after I moved to the Los Angeles area several years ago that I realized that many people were not aware that millions of victims of the Holocaust were not Jewish. Outside the Polish community, I heard very little mention about the five million non-Jewish victims -- usually referred to as "the others".

Whenever I mentioned that my parents were survivors of the Holocaust, people would look at me oddly and say, "Oh, I didn't know you were Jewish?" I realized that most people were not aware of any other Holocaust victims except Jews.

I am Jewish. I converted after taking an evening class at the University of Judaism, about a year before marrying a Jewish man. We belonged to a temple and our daughter attended religious school for many years. I love the Jewish religion and I admire the Jewish community. In no way do I want to diminish the enormous magnitude of the victimization and murder of the 5,860,000 Jewish people. The Jews were singled out by the Nazis for total extermination -- a significant fact that I do not repudiate, nor want to diminish in any way. The Jewish people have done an extraordinary job of making the younger generation around the world aware of their persecution and the immense tragedy of the Holocaust.

But what about "the others"? There were five million of them. Who were they? Whose children, whose mothers and fathers were they? How could five million human beings have been killed and forgotten?

After some research, and interviews with non-Jewish survivors, I found more information about the five million forgotten than I had ever imagined -- information that most people are not aware of. Polish citizens suffered enormously during the Holocaust -- Jews and non-Jews.

Eleven million precious lives were lost during the Holocaust of World War II. Six million of these were Polish citizens. Half of these Polish citizens were non-Jews.

While there is no argument that Hitler abhorred the Jews and caused almost six million to be ruthlessly killed, often non-Jewish victims are forgotten from Holocaust remembrances. Eleven million precious human lives were lost during the Holocaust. It would be very sad to forget even one life extinguished so ruthlessly. It would be a tragedy to forget five million. ◄►

Chapter 2 - Who Were the Others?

Of the 11 million people killed during the Holocaust, six million were Polish citizens. Three million were Polish Jews and another three million were Polish Christians and Catholics. Most of the remaining mortal victims were from other countries including Hungary, Czechoslovakia, Ukraine, Russia, Holland, France and even Germany.

First we need to examine Hitler's egocentric and maniac ideology. Hitler, who was Chancellor of Germany during the Holocaust, came to power in 1933 when Germany was experiencing severe economic hardship. Hitler promised the Germans that he would bring them prosperity and that his military actions would restore Germany to a position of power in Europe.

Hitler had a vision of a Master Race of Aryans that would control Europe. He used very powerful propaganda techniques to convince not only the German people, but countless others, that if they eliminated the people who stood in their way and the degenerates and racially inferior, they - the great Germans would prosper.

Polish Non-Jews - Hitler's First Target.

Hitler's first target was Germany's closest neighbor to the east, Poland, an agricultural country with little military power. Hitler attacked Poland from three directions on September 1, 1939 and in just over one month; Poland surrendered -- unable to defend itself against the powerful German prowess.

"All Poles will disappear from the world.... It is essential that the great German people should consider it as its major task to destroy all Poles." *Heinrich Himmler*

In Poland, Hitler saw an agricultural land in close proximity to Germany, populated by modest but strong and healthy farmers. Hitler quickly took control of Poland by specifically wiping out the Polish leading class -- the Intelligentsia. During the next few years, millions of other Polish citizens were rounded up and either placed in slave labor for German farmers and factories or taken to concentration camps where many were either starved and worked to death or used for scientific experiments.

The Jews in Poland were forced inside ghettos, but the non-Jews were made prisoners inside their own country. No one was allowed out. Many Polish men were forced to wear a patch with the letter "P" - much like the Star of David patches that their Jewish neighbors wore.

The Germans took over the ranches, farms and Polish factories. Most healthy citizens were forced into slave labor. Young Polish men were drafted into the German army. Blond haired children were "Germanized" and trained from an early age to be Nazi supporters. ▶

Jehovah Witnesses - They Stood Firm

Every European country, even Germany, had those who did not believe in the Nazi ideology and who were willing to die for their beliefs. Perhaps no other group stood so firmly in their beliefs as the Jehovah Witnesses. Hitler felt particularly threatened by this strong group of Christians because they, from the very beginning, refused to recognize any God other than Jehovah. When asked to sign documents of loyalty to the Nazi ideology, they refused.

Thousands of Jehovah Witnesses were imprisoned as "dangerous" traitors because they refused to take a pledge of loyalty to the Third Reich, refused to join the German workers union, to serve in the military or even raise their arms in the Heil Hitler salute.

Witnesses were among and earliest victims sent to concentration camps such as Sachsenhausen, Buchenwald and Ravensbruck. The Watchtower History Archive of Jehovah s Witnesses in Germany has registered over 4200 Witnesses of different nationalities who were locked up in a concentration camp. They were often considered 'voluntary prisoners', because the moment they recanted their views, they could be freed.

Those who were put into concentration camps, suffered in other ways. Forced to wear purple armbands, many lost their jobs and their pensions. Children of Jehovah's Witnesses were ridiculed by teachers, expelled by principals and bullied by their classmates. Some children were even forcibly removed from their homes and sent to orphanages or private homes to be brought up as "good Germans". ►

Rom Gypsies - Executed for Their Race

Like the Jews, the Rom Gypsies were chosen for total annihilation just because of their race. Even though Jews are defined by religion, Hitler saw the Jewish people as a race that he believed needed to be completely annihilated. Like the Jews, the Rom Gypsies also were a nomadic people that were persecuted throughout history. The Germans believed both the Jews and the Gypsies were racially inferior and degenerate and therefore worthless. Half a million Gypsies, almost the entire Eastern European Gypsy population, was wiped out by the Nazis.

But, the Gypsies who survived were ignored as Holocaust survivors and not even allowed to receive war reparations.

The Romani community has struggled to get any recognition as victims for their persecution and near-annihilation. To this day they continue to fight for commemoration. In late 2007, Romanian President, Traian Basecsu, apologized publicly for his nation's role during the Holocaust and ordered that the Porajmos (the name used by the Romani community for their Holocaust of World War II) to be taught in schools.

Today, there are at least two permanent museums, the Museum of Romani Culture in Czech Republic and the Ethnographic Museum in Poland which have exhibits memorializing the Gypsies for their losses. ►

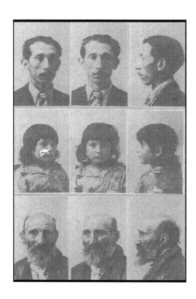

Afro-Europeans - Sterilization and Humiliation

Prior to World War I, there were very few dark-skinned people of African descent in Germany. But during World War I, black African soldiers were brought in by the French during the Allied occupation. Most of the Germans, who were very race conscious, despised the dark-skinned "invasion". Some of these black soldiers married white German women that bore children referred to as "Rhineland Bastards" or the "Black Disgrace". In Mein Kampf, Hitler said he would eliminate all the children born of African-German descent because he considered them an "insult" to the German nation.

"The mulatto children came about through rape or the white mother was a whore," Hitler wrote. "In both cases, there is not the slightest moral duty regarding these offspring of a foreign race."

The Nazis set up a secret group, Commission Number 3, to organize the sterilization of these "Rhineland Bastards" to keep intact the purity of the Aryan race. In 1937, all local authorities in Germany were to submit a list of all the mulattos. Then, these children were taken from their homes or schools without parental permission and put before the commission. Once a child was decided to be of black descent, the child was taken immediately to a hospital and sterilized. About 400 children were medically sterilized -- many times without their parents' knowledge. ▶

Homosexuals - Tagged and Tortured

Because Hitler's plan for a great Master Race had no room for any homosexuals, many males from all nations, including Germany, were persecuted, tortured and executed. Hitler even searched his own men and found suspected homosexuals that were sent to concentration camps wearing their S.S. uniforms and medals.

The homosexual inmates were forced to wear pink triangles on their clothes so they could be easily recognized and further humiliated inside the camps.

At least ten percent of the more than one million homosexual Germans were arrested under the Third Reich's anti-homosexuals laws. Others were imprisoned in government run mental hospitals. Hundreds were reportedly castrated by court order. Between 5,000 and 15,000 homosexual men were incarcerated in concentration camps, according to the International Association of Lesbian and Gay Children of Holocaust Survivors. ▶

The Disabled - Put to Death Like Cats and Dogs

The Nazis decided that it was a waste of time and money to support the disabled. During Hitler's "cleansing program", thousands of people with various handicaps were deemed useless and simply put to death like dogs and cats. It's estimated that about 400,000 were sterilized because their illnesses were regarded to be inherited. They established the T-4 Euthanasia Program in order to maintain the "purity" of the so-called Aryan race by systematically killing children and adults with physical deformities or mental illness. Between 75,000 to 250,000 people were killed from 1939 through 1941. ▸

Resisters from All Nations - Men, Women and Children

Every European nation had its courageous resisters. Poland's Underground army - made up of children, teenagers, and regular men and women - was responsible for defending the lives of thousands of its Jewish and non-Jewish citizens. Many were killed for their acts of courage against the Nazis. Even though most German citizens were supportive of Hitler's plan to control Europe, there were German citizens who died because they refused to go along with Hitler's plan.

Hitler wanted not only to conquer all of Europe, but Hitler also wanted to create a new religion and to replace Jesus Christ as a person to be worshipped. Hitler expected his followers to worship the Nazi ideology. Since Catholic priests and Christian pastors were often influential leaders in their community, they were sought out by the Nazis very early. Thousands of Catholic priests and Christian pastors were forced into concentration camps. A special barracks was set up at Dachau, the camp near Munich, Germany, for clergymen. A few survived. Some were executed, but most were allowed to die slowly of starvation or disease.

Many husbands and wives of Jews in Germany were forced to choose between divorce and concentration camps. Hitler would not allow "interracial" marriages. Those that chose to remain married were punished by imprisonment in camps where many died. ◄►

Chapter 3 - Resistance Fighter from the Underground

Most knew him as Tadeusz Borowski. Only the Polish resistance fighters knew him by his pseudonym, "Irek". As 2nd Lieutenant in the Polish Home Army, (Armia Krajowa), Irek was responsible for men with names like: "Szczur", "Ludwik", "Jurek", and "Chawcki". He took his orders from "Waligora", a.k.a. Major Jan Tarnowski, commander of Wola Region in Warsaw.

Wearing either stolen German uniforms or just plain street clothes, these homemade soldiers were the Polish Underground -- the resistance fighters of Nazi-occupied Poland. Fathers, grandfathers and young boys fought side by side with only red and white armbands for identification. They came together to defend, as best as they could, their beloved homeland. They fought with Polish pistols and German "shmyzers", automatic sub-machine guns, which they either stole or bought from the Nazis. They concealed their precious cache in cemeteries and hospital grounds.

The city sewers became their staging area, their Headquarters and their passage ways. The younger ones -- teenagers worked as liaisons, running through the sewers smuggling supplies and passing cryptic messages and orders.

"One night," says Borowski, "we got the order that our armbands must be switched before dawn from our left arms to our right arms." The Germans had infiltrated their ranks. "In the morning we were instructed to shoot anyone wearing an armband on their left arm."

Through the wet stinking sewers they moved like rats in sewage that was sometimes chest high. "We would have to dismantle our weapons," says Borowski, "and carry them along with our ammunition over our heads so they would not get wet."

In one almost comic military operation, Borowski, who speaks perfect German, dressed himself in a stolen Tirolean mountaineer's outfit -- complete with a feathered hat. With the help of three of his men, who followed discreetly in a "borrowed" German automobile, Borowski befriended three Nazi police officers. The charlatan then coyly maneuvered the German officers into a quiet cul-de-sac where his three partners were waiting.

By day Borowski worked within the walls of the Warsaw Ghetto as an engineer at the Tyton Fabryka at Dzeilna 62. Taking advantage of his freedom to pass through the well-guarded gates without suspicion, Borowski smuggled weapons, ammunition and forged documents inside for the Jewish Underground. He also worked with the Jewish Underground secretly preparing selected Jewish men and boys for combat.

Zegota was the cryptic code-name that became the word for the Polish Council of Assistance to the Jews (Rada Pomocy Żydom) established with the approval of several Polish organizations on December 4, 1942. Headquartered in Warsaw, Żegota had branches in several cities and major villages throughout Poland. Żegota aided the Jews both inside and outside the ghettos by providing forged documents, food, lodging, medicine and financial support.

With his ability to speak four languages fluently and his cunning talent for the art of war, he became a hero many times over. For his active participation in the Warsaw Ghetto uprising, and for his part in smuggling arms into the Ghetto, Borowski was awarded the Cross of Valour and The Cross of Merit with Sword. In 1948, he received the highest Medal of Honor to be bestowed on a Polish soldier, the Virtuti Militari Class V. Even 40 years later, Borowski flew to Warsaw where he was, again decorated with medals, including one inscribed, "To the Heroes of the Warsaw Ghetto 1940 - 1943."

"I risked my life to save lives," said Borowski. "I'm not looking for glory. I just want people to know the truth [about] what happened."

Pursued by the Soviet Political Police, (NKVD), after the war, Borowski left Poland in 1950. He immigrated to the United States with his wife, Helena, who had worked as a double agent in a German submarine base for the Polish Intelligence. They raised three children while Mr. Borowski worked as a design engineer for Lockheed. ◄►

Chapter 4 - Dutch Teenager in Holland

By: Grace de Rond

"I had to walk barefoot through the snow for ten hours. Others had shoes, but not me, with my size 13 feet. I was feverish and exhausted, and I could hardly breathe because I had tuberculosis and pneumonia. When I fell for the third time, I couldn't get up. The soldier pointed his gun at me and shouted, '"Get up! I'd rather kill you than leave you here for the Allies to find!'"

Toine de Rond was 17 years old when Holland surrendered to the Nazis in May 1940. He had a nice girlfriend and a bright future as an artist. Eight months later, the Nazis began deporting Dutch citizens for forced labor - able-bodied men and women to work in its factories and sustain the war effort. The profile included healthy, non-Jewish males ages 18-50 and females ages 21-35.

From 1942, razzias were conducted, where thousands of Dutch citizens were gathered from public sites such as churches, markets, and street corners. Resisters were sentenced to penal work camps called strafarbeitslagers.

Between 1939 and 1945, the Nazis abducted more than ten million people from the defeated countries. According to the Red Cross, more than 500,000 of these were Dutch citizens. More than 30,000 of them died in camps.

It is mid-June, and Spring 2003 has been uncommonly beautiful in Holland, with record sunshine in March. Outside Toine's flat in a suburb of Rotterdam, it is still daylight at 9pm. In his darkish living room, Toine speaks reluctantly about what happened to him 60 years ago. He would rather talk about his favorite subjects: sports, or his son, Ron, and 13 year-old granddaughter, Zosha. Toine's only daughter, Marlo, died seven years ago of a brain hemorrhage.

Toine is an attractive man, 6'2" and slender, with a firm handshake and an engaged look. His long graying hair is combed straight back from his high forehead. An early family photo of him at age 40 reveals the same soft mouth and intent eyes. Then and now, he expresses a wounded strength.

Though Toine speaks animatedly, his voice remains level, his tone pragmatic. He plants his feet on the floor, his elbows on his knees, and gestures continuously with his big hands, jabbing his fingers at the air like a professor waving not one, but two long pointers.

"At first, I was able to avoid the war. But in 1943, during the big razzias, the ground got too hot under my feet, so I escaped to Antwerp to live with relatives. When the war came close to Antwerp, I moved to another family in Paris. There I was fine for a while, until I learned that my mother had suffered a nervous breakdown. I decided to return to Holland. In November, when crossing the border from France to Belgium, I was captured for the first time."

During the fall of 1943, Toine was held in several prisons. He escaped from one, but an English-speaking person betrayed him by first gaining his trust and then returning him to the Nazis for a bounty.

"On December 3, 1943, I was transported to Siegen, Germany to work in a machine factory. The treatment was bearable, but we never heard anything from the outside world. Eventually, I found a way around that through a German family in Siegen. I could live there as long as I showed up for work every day. This family owned a radio, so I listened to Radio Oranje. And daily, I conveyed the news to my co-workers who were mostly French, Russian, Polish, and Dutch.

"Of course, not to the Germans!" he adds grinning.

"Often, I had to tell the workers to be careful, because sometimes when the news was good they looked suspiciously happy. Everything went well, and optimism returned due to the good news on the radio. Although it was risky to listen to the news and spread the messages in the lion's den, I couldn't resist doing it because it was for a good cause."

When the Dutch government organized itself in exile in London, it sought a way to maintain contact with its citizens under occupation. The officials asked the British Broadcasting Corporation for transmitting time, and on July 28, 1940, Radio Oranje aired for the first time. Queen Wilhelmina spoke regularly to support the people back home. Jetty Pearl sang a popular cabaret song: "After rain always comes sunshine. After these dark days of high-handedness, disgrace, and terror, there will come a day of joy and reunion. We are proud and full of courage, because the people of Holland will persevere. The small country of Holland is fighting like a giant."

Radio Oranje was so popular with the Dutch people that the Nazis confiscated all their radios. Resisters were sentenced to the strafarbeitslagers.

"Unfortunately, just after the news of Normandy aired, my so-called freedom ended. I can still see myself running like a rabbit to my co-workers to tell them the great news of the Allied invasion. What a joy we felt!"

Toine's "so-called freedom" ended when several of his countrymen betrayed him. When confronted by guards, the Dutch workers responded that they had heard the news from "de Rond, who listens to the radio every day." At that point, Toine's circumstances worsened.

"What a terrible time, not knowing what would happen, just waiting for the verdict. I was kept in solitary confinement for three months. When I was finally taken to the court, the accusations against me were read aloud. Everything I said in my defense was ignored, while the 'witnesses' were believed. I still remember their names. Later, I learned that they had defected for money.

"The verdict was three years of hard labor in a strafarbeitslager - for listening to, and spreading info from, an 'enemy' radio broadcast."

Paintings hang in every room of Toine's flat, as well as in his ex-wife's flat where he still has dinner once a week, with her and her partner. Toine has painted all his life, mostly oil copies of masterpieces. His talent has been a god-send to a difficult life, especially since age forty-five, when he had his first heart attack and had to go on permanent disability.

Twilight is finally settling in, now that it is almost 10:30pm. Toine's shoulders droop only slightly as he rolls another cigarette and recalls his most difficult experiences. In October 1944, he was transported to the penal work camp at Frondenberg. He explains that after his trial, he was treated as an animal, what the Nazis called an Untermensch or subhuman.

"A lot of beatings, very little and poor food, inadequate clothes and shoes, and long, unbearable labor. I tried to escape, but I was caught and put in a special detention group where the guard was even more abusive. He would beat us with a bat, the butt of his rifle, or with stones. Whatever pleased the sadist. More than once he knocked me unconscious. There were sadists everywhere.

"I was put to slave labor in several prisons. I've done very hard labor in a stinking leather factory, a stone quarry in the mountains, a bomb shell factory, in steel mills where the ovens were too hot and still they made us keep working, carrying railroad ties to bombed railroad sites. Since I was the tallest in the group and therefore carrying most of the weight on my shoulders, I would sometimes collapse, but they would beat me until I got up again."

In his book, Inside the Vicious Heart, Robert H. Abzug describes a phenomenon called "double vision," which allows people to repress their emotions and become numb when faced with an individual's suffering through the hands of another. Allied soldiers experienced it when they liberated the camps in 1945 and could not comprehend what they saw. General George Patton purportedly ran behind a building to be sick. General Dwight Eisenhower radioed Washington that the "unspeakable conditions" were worse than anything yet reported.

The winter of 1944-45 was extremely severe for Holland. The Nazis blocked food shipments to the country, driving Dutch citizens to eat tulip bulbs to survive. People died of starvation in the streets.

As Allied troops grew closer in Spring 1945, Toine was moved from camp to camp. The Nazis raced to stay ahead of the approaching armies, forcing their emaciated and sick, often dying prisoners on death marches.

"I spent March, 1945 at a camp in Munster. By then, I was very sick. 31 March was our last transport. We had to leave because the Allies were close. We had to march 14 hours to a prison in Klarholz. I was so sick that after 10 hours of walking I collapsed. I had fallen twice before, but with some severe beatings I was chased back to my feet. The third time, I couldn't get up because I couldn't breathe anymore."

The Nazis stuck sharp objects in the soles of the feet of men and women who had collapsed, to determine whether they were faking. Toine explains that as he lay in the snow for the third time, he resolved himself to remain still.

"The soldier in charge thought I was faking and was convinced that I wanted to stay behind to be rescued by the Allies. He pointed his gun at me and shouted, 'Get up!' What a terrible moment that was. I was sure I would die.

"This last transport would have meant the end for me if not for the Regierungsrat, the head of the camp who was walking with us. He saved my life when he said, 'Why don't you just toss him on the cart and we'll deal with him when we get to Klarholz.' "They did. And when we finally got to Klarholz, I escaped from the cart and hid in the barracks, behind the beds of the other prisoners. This is where I spent two days and nights."

Occasionally, as Toine tells his story, a roguish grin comes over his face. Then it is possible to still see the doggedness of a young man forced to mature quickly under impossible circumstances - yet still defiant, and eventually exhilarated, to win over an adversary too evil to comprehend. He grins in just such a way when he explains that he always referred to the Nazis as 'die herren,' the gentlemen.

"Die Herren didn't have much time for me anyway because the Allies were close, and they were too busy running in an effort to save themselves. At least that's what they thought!

"There he was, about 10:00am, an American officer, standing feet widespread, hands stuck casually in his pockets, a sten gun slung over his shoulder, on the threshold of our barracks. Now it was quickly over for the ones who ruled us. I can still see them trembling on their legs, 13 Nazi officers facing only one American! They were all arrested!

"On 9 April, we returned to our Fatherland where I was diagnosed with pneumonia and tuberculosis. My weight was 56 kilos where normally I was 85. Eventually, I had surgery on my lungs, and also on the injuries to my back from the beatings. On 22 June, I was finally brought home. My parents, my six older brothers, and my sister - everyone was safe!"

After several operations and hospital stays, Toine spent five more years in sanatoriums - resting, retreating, and healing. But how does one heal from such an ordeal?

As Toine considers the question, he rises from his leather armchair to switch on several lamps, creating a glow that wards off the thick darkness outside. Gezellig is the word used by all Nederlanders to describe a warm, safe, lamp lit household. As he settles in his chair again, his words provide some clues to his recovery.

"It was a religious time. I'd been raised as a Catholic. Someone gave me a bidprentje [a small prayer-picture] of Beuron's Pieta. I loved that piece of work and decided to recreate it as a mosaic. It helped me pass the time."

Toine explains that he never actually finished the work, which stood in his basement for 50 years and now hangs in his son's home. The full work by Beuron is meticulously penciled to scale on the 2'x4' board, but only the two figures are completely filled in with tiny colored tiles. Toine's choice of theme is significant: the power of life over death, a wounded son in his mother's arms.

Perhaps life itself provides spurs to heal. In 1943, when the English-speaking person betrayed Toine, he swore he would never speak English again. He kept that promise for 50 years, until his son married an American woman. To communicate with her, he had to break his vow.

Two years ago, Toine ran into an old friend, the girlfriend from when he was seventeen. Today, as nighttime settles over Toine's rooms and paintings, they are once again sweethearts, and hopefully able to reclaim some of what was lost - still exhilarated to have won over evil in the end. ◄►

Chapter 5 - The Diary of Number 1067

By: Zygfried Baginski

I weighed 220 pounds before I was apprehended by the German Gestapo in Poland in 1944. After ten months of incarceration, I weighed 72 pounds, my hair had turned gray, and I was never the same again. I witnessed incredulous inhumanity, bestiality, starvation, floggings, and extreme cruelty. Trying to recall these events is very distressing -- even 50 some years later. But, I will try.

I was apprehended in a routine roundup, along with several other men and boys. We were placed in buildings surrounded by barbed wire. The police immediately went to our houses and ransacked our families' homes, tore up the floors, and destroyed furniture trying to find any kind of hidden weapons or any evidence at all so they would have an excuse to execute us.

Three days later we were forced inside railroad boxcars -- 40 men to a car. We were given no food or water. A bucket in the corner was our toilet. The only food we had was that which was given us by our anxious families.

We traveled in the stuffy and smelly boxcars for at least three days and nights. At the end of our trip, we were ordered to walk for a several hours until we reached Gross-Rosen K.Z. [K.Z was the acronym for "concentration camp" in English from the German word Konzentrationslager.] German SS soldiers with their yelping and growling dogs closely guarded us. There were a few hundred of us. We were lined up in a large open area and told to strip off our clothes and place them in neatly folded piles. Then all of our clothes were confiscated.

One by one, we were strip-searched. Then our heads and our genital areas were shaved. Some men were ordered to have their genital areas swabbed with a strong disinfectant that burned like fire. One man cried out in pain and was hit in the face so hard that his nose bled.

We were then issued striped clothing and wooden shoes. We had to exchange clothes among ourselves to try to find some that fit. We were each assigned a number and given two cloth patches with the number on them. My number was 1067. These were to be sewn onto our clothing, one on the jacket and one on the pants. I received a patch with the letter "P" on it that identified me as being Polish.

One day, soon after our arrival, five men were called: Sosnowski, who was a hunchback; Kosmaczewski, who had become mentally unstable; Formeister, who was very overweight, and two others whose names I do not remember. These five men were taken away. We never saw them again.

On another day, I saw six men -- kapos - -chained to one another. They were following an SS man. Behind them was another kapo who was beating them with a chain. I later learned that these six kapos were involved in a scuffle during a card game the previous night that resulted in one man being killed. Now these men were being punished, first with a beating and then death. [Kapos were inmates whom the SS chose to carry out their orders and keep track of the others.]

I spent about a week at Gross-Rosen before I was transferred, along with several others, to Aslau K.Z. There was a military airport nearby and we were given jobs in one of the hangars. Every morning before work, we were ordered to line up to be counted. This usually took a long time because we had to remain standing until everyone was accounted for.

We were hungry and tired and very weak almost the entire time. It was an enormous chore just to keep moving until the end of the day. In the evening we lined up to be counted again. Any person accused of breaking any work rules was called forward and punished. Either they were hit in the face, given a beating or they were ordered to run until they fell from exhaustion. This last form of punishment was called "sport" and was a form of entertainment for the SS men.

One morning two men were missing. We were ordered to remain standing until the two were found. We stood for six hours. Finally the SS men with dogs found the escapees. They were transferred to the main camp, probably to the Punishment Commando. They were never seen again.

Another time, a man was discovered in a tunnel that had been dug under the barbed wire fence. The entire camp was lined up to witness his punishment. He was given 100 lashes. After 30 lashes he lost consciousness and fell to the ground. The SS men threw water on him and a kapo named Eric gave him 70 more lashes. The guy never screamed or cried out. It was terrifying to watch. Unbelievably, this man survived this horrendous beating. Some months later he showed us his wounds on his buttocks. There was no skin. The flesh was red. There were two open wounds about the size of a half-dollar where the bones were visible. Red and blue veins branched out form the center of the wound.

Sunday was a day of rest from our work. On some Sundays, the entire barracks was ordered to take a bath. Buckets of water were heated up on a wood burning stove. The heated water was poured into a large tub. The first one to bathe was the leader of the barracks. Next, the members of his team took their turn in the bath. Finally, all 300 of us were ordered to bathe in the same water. I tried to keep my head above the polluted water, but the guards physically shoved my head under. I remember shutting my eyes, and mouth and trying to hold my nose so none of the putrid water would seep inside.

One day while standing in line, I noticed a man collapse some distance away from me but in the same line. He fell against the man next to him knocking him over. We were so weak that when this man fell, one by one, like dominos, the entire line of men began falling down. I saw what has happening and I tried to step out of the way, but I was so weak that I could not move fast enough and I too went down. The SS men and the kapos found this very amusing.

In November 1944, a new SS officer arrived. We called him "Croat". He decided to double our shift, which created a 16-hour workday. In the morning we received a cup of Erzart coffee that was impossible to drink. Most of us used it as warm water to wash our hands and faces. Later in the day we would get one liter of watery green vegetable soup and a small piece of black bread. The soup tasted terrible, but we ate because we were starving.

Because it was so late when we returned to our barracks at the end of the workday, our "dinner" would be set aside for us outside in metal bowls. During the winter, the top layer of the soup would freeze and we would have to break the ice to eat it. We went straight to bed after eating because we were exhausted. My legs ached so much from all the walking, standing and working, that I lost all feeling in my feet.

Meals That Dogs Would Refuse

Sometime after Christmas 1944, we were evacuated from Aslau. We were ordered to load about ten farm wagons with supplies. We then pushed and steered the wagons across the countryside on a journey that took several days. Anyone who was unable to walk or who collapsed from exhaustion was shot and killed on the spot.

One night two prisoners escaped. The commandant was so angry that he punished all of us by asking five men standing next to me to step out of line and move behind a building. Then we listened while he shot them with his gun. To this day I do not understand how I escaped not being chosen that night. We arrived in Nordhausen K.Z. in March 1943 where we stayed for a few days only. Then we marched to Dora.

Hospital without Medical Supplies

It was about this time that I got sick. A gland in my neck was so swollen that it locked my jaw and my teeth were clenched tight. My commander noticed my condition and sent me to the hospital. It was called a hospital but hardly anyone left this building alive. There were no medical supplies - just very sick and dying people. One man had gangrene in his arm. Three times they amputated parts of his arm without anesthesia. He finally died.

There were about 600 patients in the hospital when I arrived. In a few weeks four hundred of these were dead and any patient well enough to walk was sent back to work.

Liberty at Last

One morning we looked out the window and noticed that all the SS guards were gone. The Wermacht had replaced them. A few days later, General Patton's Army arrived at the camp. I remember the first Allied soldier I saw was an African-American smiling and throwing chocolate candy bars and Camel cigarettes to us through the window. We were liberated. ◄►

Chapter 6 - American Citizen and Holocaust Survivor

By: Susan Ost-Perrone

I have never written about this subject before. I have hardly even talked about it. I guess I never felt that we, non-Jews, also "owned" the tragedies of the Holocaust. The Internet site (www.holocaustforgotten.com) enlightened me to realize that it wasn't just Jews that were treated horribly. Until I visited this site, I had always thought that it was just a miserable mistake that my family got caught up in an atrocity that was happening to the Jews.

My father, until I asked him, never talked about how his family was torn apart by the Holocaust in Poland. I only knew bits and pieces of stories I had heard when my parents talked quietly. After visiting this site on the non-Jewish victims and survivors, I was inspired to talk to my father and ask him more specific questions.

My father, George T. Ost, (formerly Ostrowski) was born in Milwaukee, Wisconsin in 1918, just after his parents emigrated from Poland. George was the youngest of seven children. Sometime soon after George was born, his mother returned to Poland with the children. His father continued to live in the United States to support the family. George and his brother, Edward were U.S. Citizens, but the rest of the family members were Polish Citizens. All the children were educated and raised as Catholics in Gdynia, Poland.

Living in Poland when Germany invaded in 1939, George was drafted into the Polish Army although he was an

American citizen. Being college-educated, the Polish army offered him immediate officership. A few weeks later his entire troop was captured by the Nazi's. George was beat unconscious with a rifle butt. His teeth were knocked out. He awoke on a truck, bleeding and bruised, thinking he was headed for the forest to be executed. Instead, he and 32 other Polish soldiers were taken to a nearby concentration camp. When the Germans learned he was a Lieutenant he was treated a little better, but they did not believe he was a U.S. Citizen.

When George's mother learned of his capture, she immediately began searching for him. Mrs. Ostrowski found her youngest son in a concentration camp, 14 miles from Gdynia. She talked to the Nazi officers and was able to convince them that he was an American citizen. He was released along with four other young men from his troop six weeks before the United States' involvement in the war. George was lucky. Unfortunately not everyone is his family was so lucky.

A few weeks later, George and his brother, Edward, who had just returned from fighting in the Polish Army at the Russian border, were walking into town to register Edward's return to Gdynia. The Nazis required all Polish citizens to be registered. George and the other members of his family had already registered. While waiting in the long slow-moving line with Edward, George decided to leave to buy some cigarettes. Unfortunately, when he returned, the entire line of people, along with his brother was gone. No one knows exactly what happened.

Edward was 24 years old. They never saw him alive again. In 1944 or 1945, George's two sisters, Sophia and Hatti, identified Edward's' remains in a mass grave in the woods not far from Gdynia. He was traced by tattooed numbers.

After the United States became involved in the war it was necessary for George to leave Poland. He headed for Marseilles, France where he embarked on a boat to the United States. George tried to get settled in the U.S. but was soon drafted into the United States Army. He was part of the Army Air Corp., which later was to become the Air Force. George was almost court-martialed for being a spy because he spoke fluent German. After that was straightened out, the Army sent George back to Europe to fight the Germans.

Fortunately, he was not captured this time and returned home after the war to marry and start a family. George Ost passed away in March 2004 surrounded by his family. He was very touched to think that anybody cared about his story. ◄►

Chapter 7 - Kidnapped and Deported

By: Joseph S. Wardzala

More than one million Poles were deported to forced labor camps in Nazi Germany. There are no books, nor data showing the number of people who were murdered in those camps. Those who survived remember how cruelly they were treated. I am one of them. I have lost my young years and health over there.

When Germany started the war, they mobilized every young German into the Nazi armed forces. There was a shortage of laborers at home. At first, they appealed to Poles to go and work in Germany. Some Poles went, since they had no means to survive in Occupied Poland. Later, the Germans applied forced deportation for work. They kidnapped young men and women in the street, in the marketplace, and in front of churches on Sundays. Special camps were set up for Poles, separate ones for men and others for women.

I was kidnapped on a street in Tarnow in April 1941, pushed into a goods wagon and transported to Germany. Three days later, the train stopped in Braunschwieg. We were told to leave the wagon. Here we were met by other Germans who were choosing people for work they needed done.

I was assigned to work for a firm that was building underground shelters for Germans in the neighborhood of Wattenstadt, where a huge Herman Goering factory was located. The work was exhausting, 10 hours a day; six days a week, often even on Sundays. Older people were dying of exhaustion. The camp was surrounded with barbed wire. It was administered by Germans. Every morning we were divided into groups and led to work under strict supervision. After work, a bowl of soup and microscopic cube of margarine and bread was given. This was the only meal for the day. We felt hunger all day long. Every morning, we were so exhausted that we could hardly move. A brown leather whip was used to make people work faster.

We were liberated by the American Army in April 1945. Displaced Person Camps were created and organized. Now, children were able to begin their education in schools in the camps. On Sundays we were finally able to attend the Holy Mass. People were given jobs. We lived in the same barracks as during the war. Some people lived in the previously military buildings. I taught school and worked in the office of a Polish Displaced Persons Camp, organized scouting, and helped the priests in the chapel.

I arrived in the United States in 1950, and settled in Derby, Connecticut. Since 1966, I have been organizing exhibits and showing films, spreading information about Polish history and culture. In 1990, thanks to the Kosciuszko Foundation of New York, I was invited by the Holocaust Committee to Washington, D.C. to describe my experience in the Nazi camp. The interview was recorded and may be seen on video in the Holocaust Memorial Museum in Washington D.C.

I gave the museum my documents showing my work as a forced laborer in Nazi Germany: my identity card, food stamps (which showed my number and date with large "P" in the background). A part of the stamp was to be turned into the kitchen to obtain a meal. Every Pole had to have the letter "P" sewn on their clothing. It was forbidden for Poles to ride in busses, trains, to enter a restaurant or theater. My letter "P" can be seen in the Holocaust Museum. ◄►

Chapter 8 - French Survivor of Nordhuesen

By: Michel Depierre and Peter Branton

I was born July 22, 1926 (72 years old when I wrote this) at Villers-Vermont (Oise) France. I was the oldest son of 10 children. Lived the first 10 years on farms at villers-Vermont until 8 years old then at St Samson La Poterie until 10 years old with my grandmothers and parents. Then I family moved to Noyon where I still reside. From 1936 to 1940 attended primary school in Noyon and then started working to help out the family. From 1940 to 1944 worked in a factory.

Joined the Resistance Movement to Fight the Germans

On June 6, 1944 (D-Day), I joined, in the forest near Noyon, the "Maquis des Usages" (resistance movement) to fight the Germans. I recycled weapons, grenades, and guns. Reception of British parachutes. Also I gave aid to British and American Aviators that were shot down.

On June 23, 1944 "Le Maquis" (The resistant team) was attacked by the Germans. Two resistance fighters were killed but we killed 6 German soldiers. The fight was tough. With our machine guns (British machine guns called STEN) we won over the 40 German soldiers, when there were only twelve of us. Two of us were only 17 years old. We were in a hunting chalet surrounded by the Germans that we had to repel to escape.

We took the opportunity, after they retreated in a truck, to escape and walk 15 km in the forest. The next day the Germans came back and bombed the chalet. The Gestapo organized a manhunt, so we took refuge in huge underground caves.

Arrested

On returning to Noyon to inform my family, the Gestapo arrested me on July 20th, 1944. They took me to the Prison of Compiegne where I was questioned and tortured. On August 16th, 1944 we were moved to the camp of Royallieu near Compiegne, where other resistance fighters were gathered from all over France. 55,000 resistance fighters left Compiegne during the war for concentration camps in Germany.

The next day August 17th, 1944, we are locked in animal wagons (80-90 persons per wagon) in Compiegne forest. Our destination is the concentration camp of Buchenwald where we arrived 92 hours later, completely dehydrated. It was during August in an incredible heat, we received only a 1/4 liter of water during the trip. People were dying, others were losing their mind. Some of them were leeching the water condensation on the steel at night. For the toilette facility only a metallic bucket in the middle of the wagon with an unbearable odor, was available.

We arrived at Buchenwald exhausted on August 21st, 1944. Strong people became, in 92 hours, very old. We slept for three weeks outside on the garbage heap of the" big Camp". We were shaved from head to toe and given striped uniforms.

300 Prisoners were Killed

August 23rd, 1944 the camp of Buchenwald was bombed by the Allies. The factory near the camp and 58 barracks

(Headquarters) were destroyed. Not too much damage in the camp but three hundred prisoners (deportees) were killed.

Towards September 10th, 1944 I was sent via "Transport Train" towards the Dutch border. We crossed Cologne (Koln), went down the Rhine towards Koblenz. The Allies are progressing so fast that we could not leave the wagons and the train was forced to return to Buchenwald. The Germans only took food for the one way trip so, on the way back we traveled three days without anything to eat.

Two days later I got really depressed when I learned that I'm leaving For the Camp of Dora (Nordhausen) to work in the underground Factory of the 'Mittelbau where we built the VI and V2 rockets. Only dead comes back from Dora in Wagons and trucks to be burned in the crematorium of Buchenwald.

A Cruel Hell

From September 15th 1944 to the beginning of April 1945 I was in the cruelest Hell. Twelve hours per day or night (eighteen hours when we rotate team) we must carry on our back extremely heavy equipment in and out of the tunnel With almost nothing in our stomach, under the rain, snow, mud, in extremely cold weather, clothed in a poor outfit, wood clogs with fabric on top which get hooked in everything and under the beatings of the "55" and "Kapos" (Often ex criminals just out of jail).

I touch the bottom of misery and mental distress. Although, I had a strong constitution from a very athletic life, my health declined rapidly. I was admitted at the "Revier" (nursery) toward March 15th 1945 for complication to a wound received in the temple by a kapos. From then on, my health became worse with numerous diseases one after the other: Pleuresie, Lymphangite, dysentrie, etc... (I don't know the English translation of those diseases).

April 3rd and 6th evacuation of Camp Dora. People in charge of the "Revier" wanted to evacuate us right away; they said that everything will be destroyed with flame throwers. With my extreme weakness I tried to go down on the Appel Plaza. But when I see the poor people in front of me being beat with tool handles, I hide behind a barracks and go back in the block where the nurse immediately sent me back out. So, I went around the Block and pushed a window that thank God opened. I'm in an empty room and my Heart is beating really fast. I collapse and lose consciousness.

Prisoners Burned to Death

When I finally regained consciousness I saw the town of Nordhausen burning about 7 km away. It was only when I came back to France that I learned that the "SS" put thousand of prisoners (Deportees) incapable of working in their barracks. The allies thought they were bombing a military installation. Around 1500 prisoners (Deportees) were killed.

On the 7th or 8th of April, the "SS" abandoned Dora except for a few dying prisoners (Deportees) like me. The camp is evacuated. We stayed a few days in this "no man's land". On April 11th, 1945 The American Army investigated the tunnel and the Camp of Dora. Shocked, they discovered about a hundred men dying in the Revier (nursery). The first military man that I saw was a Canadian Captain who spoke French. They distributed some food. It was so good, since we were dying of hunger for the last nine months. Only skin was left on our bones.

April 19th, 1945, we had gained a little more strength so they walked us to the airfield of Nordhausen. There Dakotas (Airplanes) brought supplies to the Front. American military set up tents. There is on tables some beautiful white bread, but nobody to care for us. Maybe to avoid diseases? But also because of the war they didn't have time for us. They let us sleep outside, fortunately, it didn't rain. I lay down on the workshop of a demolished building.

On April 20th, 1945 a Dakota took us from Nordhausen to "Le Bourget" Airport near Paris, where Parisian people discover what deportation is. On April 21th, 1945 I returned to my house in Noyon by train. I am very tired. It will take me several months to recover. For more than 15 years I had nightmares every night.

I got married on December 19, 1946. We had four children, two died. We have today Jean-Marc, and Sophie, who married a U.S. Marine from in Oceanside, California. Today, I'm 72 years old. I'm retired after working 50 years. 37 and a half years in Civil Service (Travaux Publics de l'Etat).

Thank you for the courageous and brave American Soldiers who came to rescue us. Without them I would not be able, 54 years later, to write these lines. Honors to those who gave their life to make this possible. ◄►

Chapter 9 - The Righteous Gentiles - Heroes and Heroines

"In front of you the Righteous I bow." Chaim Chefer

No other event in current history created so many stories of atrocities and horror as the Holocaust. Much has been written on the victimization of millions and the senseless murder of 11 million human beings. It is rare to find any sliver of goodness during that horrible time in history. Yet there are incredible stories of courage and humanity that are just beginning to be told. For many reason the heroes of these stories have not talked about their experiences. Only now, as many have aged to near extinction, they are beginning to talk -- coerced by second generation survivors who crave to hear their stories of valor.

Just as we should never forget the horrors of the Holocaust, we should also never forget the heroes of the Holocaust. There is perhaps more of a lesson in the story of the rescuers -- the heroes than even in the atrocities. Most of the victims unfortunately had no control -- no choice in their destiny. The rescuers, on the other hand, had choices. They could have chosen to have looked the other way -- as many around the world did. But not the heroes. The heroes made a decision. They chose to risk their own lives, their family's, and they often risked their homes and their own comfort to help save thousands of Jews.

At the Yad Vashem Holocaust Memorial Center in Jerusalem, there is a section called: Righteous of the Nations, set up in 1953 to honor the rescuers. As of January 2011, Yad Vashem has recognized 23,788 Righteous

Among the Nations from 45 countries. This in no way represents the entire list of rescuers. Some countries will not allow names of rescuers to be reported. Yad Vashem will only accept names of Righteous Gentiles, as they are called, when there are witness testimonies to prove the rescue. Yad Vashem admits that many times the Jewish person died even with the assistance.

For every rescuer there were many anonymous accomplices -- people who helped, but who chose to remain anonymous. The anonymous accomplices would leave packages of food or supplies on a doorstep in the middle of the night. The anonymous accomplices would give a signal when a Nazi soldier approached. Many were accomplices just by remaining silent -- by not saying anything, even when they knew that their punishment could be torture or execution. ◄►

Chapter 10 - Jan Karski - "Masterpiece of Courage"

By: John Millrany

The story of Jan Karski is best told through his photographic memory for which he has been acknowledged: what he saw in the Big Eye of history—as horrific as it was—and what he did about it.

He was born Jan Kozielewski on April 24, 1914, the youngest of eight children of Stefan and Walentyna Kozielewski. The family thrived in Lodz, Poland. They were all patriotic Roman Catholics, living in Poland's second-largest city at a time when political events roiled the nation and, inevitably, most of the civilized world.

Early on it became apparent that Jan would excel in school, an aptitude that would target him as a recruit for the diplomatic service. In short order he secured plum assignments in London and Paris. Prior, he had enlisted in the Polish army and become a decorated cavalry officer in 1939, the year German soldiers, followed in a matter of weeks by Russian troops, invaded Poland in a prelude to Hitler's "Final Solution" and the Holocaust.

The unkindest of years, 1939 resulted in the Germans walling off the main Jewish sectors of the capital of Warsaw, entrapping about 500,000 Jews in the Warsaw Ghetto. This was prelude to the choking off of food supplies, and the confinees began dying from hunger and disease. By 1942, the mass deportations of Jews were underway, with as many as 10,000 victims per day transported to Umschlagplatz Square in the Ghetto to board trains destined for the extermination camps.

Meanwhile, captured by Soviet forces, he was sent to a detention camp, but directly escaped, leading to his joining the Polish Underground. His escape proved serendipitous indeed, for most of his fellow Polish officers imprisoned with him were ultimately executed by the equally ruthless Soviets.

His next dubious encounter was at the hands of the Gestapo while on assignment in Slovakia in 1940. The imprisonment led to Jan's attempted suicide when he decided to slash his wrists following his torture by German thugs. Jan simply was fearful of giving up secrets to the enemy. However, Jan survived and was saved through hospitalization. Once again, he rebounded through escape, abetted by an underground commando.

Another signal event occurred in late August 1942 when Jan appeared in the cellar of an apartment housed in the notorious Aryan side of the Ghetto to meet with a young proponent of the Jewish Combat Organization, a nascent secret organization being developed in the Ghetto. From then on, Jan became an up-close-and-personal witness to unspeakable hardships rendered to the population. He never turned down an important assignment and became an efficient infiltrator.

Jan's first visit to the United States was imminent; arriving on U.S. soil two months after the remaining Jews in the Ghetto had an uprising. There eventuated a three-week struggle that history pegged the Warsaw Ghetto Uprising— as more than 10,000 Jews were killed in the fighting or perished in fires set by the Germans. The upshot: some 56,000 remaining Jews were hustled to the Treblinka death camp.

Jan's first-hand reports of the tragedies in Poland had faint resonance. "Almost every individual was sympathetic," Jan related, "to my reports concerning the Jews. But when I reported to the leaders of governments (including a secret meeting with President Roosevelt), they disregarded their conscience, their personal feelings. They provided a rationale which seemed valid. What was the situation? The Jews were totally helpless. The war strategy was the defeat of Germans and the defeat of Germany's war potential for all eternity. Nothing could interfere with the military crushing of the Third Reich. The Jews had no country, no government. They were fighting but they had no identity."

Jan had plans to return to Warsaw to continue his behind-the-scenes skullduggery, but was informed by his superiors that his cover had been blown to the Germans, and he was ordered to stay put.

Mercifully, by 1945 the war had ended, along with the government in exile Jan had served. So it was, at the age of 39, Jan was accepted by the School of Foreign Service at Georgetown University. In less than three years he received his doctorate and continued at Georgetown as a teacher until 1984.

A naturalized citizen (1954), Jan married Pola Nirenska (nee) Nirensztajn), a Polish-born dancer and choreographer. The daughter of an observant Jewish father, her many relatives were killed in the Holocaust—a too-often story old—but fortunately survived after arriving in London.

Jan died in July 2000 at the age of 86.

In the book, *KARSKI: How One Man Tried to Stop the Holocaust* (John Wiley & Sons, Inc.), authors E. Thomas Wood and Stanislaw Jankowski noted in their Preface:

"The patient cooperation of Professor Jan Karski and his wife, Pola Nirenska, made this book possible. Not only did Professor Karski open his personal archive to us, endure many full days of questioning, and painstakingly review the

manuscript for accuracy, but he and his wife also offered
bed and board to both authors on numerous occasions. We
profoundly regret that Mrs. Karski did not live to see this
book. The authors dedicate this book to Professor Jan
Karski, and to the memory of Pola Mirenska Karski, with
heartfelt gratitude and admiration."

In his Foreword to the book, Elie Wiesel, the famed
founder of the eponymous Foundation for Humanity,
captured the essence of Jan Karski:

"Was his life a great story? It was more than that: it is a
masterpiece of courage, integrity, and humanism.

"How can one fail to admire this great Pole—great in every
sense of the word-who dared to reveal and condemn the
anti-Semitism that prevailed in various chauvinistic groups
of the Polish underground—this fervent Catholic who
risked his life to protect millions of Jews destined to perish
in death camps that the Germans had established in his
county? Obsessed by their tragedy, he became unable to
think of anything else. He spoke of it to everyone he was
able to meet—statesmen politicians, journalists, diplomats-
—on his travels. Some refused to listen to him, others to
believe him. From General Sikorski to Anthony Eden, from
President Roosevelt to Justice Frankfurter, he recounted to
each the life and death of the Warsaw Ghetto, the death
trucks, the sealed freight cars going to Auschwitz, the fear
and hunger, the loneliness and agony of men, women, and
children whom the so-called civilized world had abandoned
and forgotten. Then he stopped. He realized that his words
were of no avail. People were busy with other things,
leaders had other priorities. I believe that this was the most
depressing timed for Jan Karski. He must have felt useless.

"But his testimony remains fruitful. Thanks to him, we
know that the individual, if he so desires, is capable of
having an effect on history. When the Allies raised their

voices on behalf of the Jews of Budapest, very, very late, in the summer of 1944, it was because men like Jan Karski knew how to penetrate their consciences.

"Jan Karski's human and humanistic message had a significance that neither the flow of time nor the forces of evil could erase or mitigate.

"Thanks to him, more than one generation continues to believe in humanity."

Twelve years after his death, in April 2012, Jan was lionized by President Barack Obama, who posthumously bestowed on Jan Karski the Presidential Medal of Freedom. In a White House press release, it was noted that the former officer in the Polish Underground "was among the first to provide eye-witness accounts of the Holocaust to the world.

The Medal of Freedom is the Nation's highest civilian honor, presented to individuals who have made especially meritorious contributions to the security or national interests of the United States, to world peace, or to cultural or other significant private endeavors." ◄►

Chapter 11 - Żegota and Irena Sendler

Żegota, also known as the Konrad Żegota Committee, was the cryptonym for the clandestine underground organization that provided assistance to the Jewish people living in Nazi-occupied Poland. Rada Pomocy Żydom, as it was called in Polish, was run by the Polish Government in Exile and was organized by both Jews and non-Jews from numerous underground political parties.

Żegota helped to save about 4,000 Polish Jews by providing food, medical care, money and false identification documents. Żegota played a large part in placing Jewish children with foster families and orphanages and church institutions. In Warsaw, Żegota's children department was run by Irena Sendler, who managed the placement of approximately 2,500 of the 9,000 Jewish children smuggled out of the Warsaw Ghetto.

Many members of Żegota were memorialized in Israel in 1963 with a planting of a tree in the Avenue of the Righteous at Yad Vashem.

Irena Sendlerowa
Head of the Childrens Section

Żegota appointed Irena Sendler, a Polish social worker, the head of its children's department. When the Nazis began destroying the Warsaw ghetto when the Nazis began destroying the Warsaw ghetto, Irena Sendler started a large-scale campaign to rescue the children who lived there. A total of 2,500 children were saved, brought out of the ghetto and hidden in Polish families, orphanages and monasteries. They received false identities and other help. In 1943, the Gestapo arrested Sendler, tortured her and sentenced her to death.

The Żegota council managed to bribe German guards and have Sendler released, and until the end of the war, she lived under a false name. After 1945, she worked at the social welfare department of Warsaw, contributing to the establishment of orphanages and rest homes for those who had lost their families in the war. Sendler also managed the department of medical education at the Ministry of Health, where she put forward an initiative to open high schools for girls who wanted to become nurses.

In 1983, the Israeli Yad Vashem institute honored Sendler with the Righteous Among the Nations medal, and in 2003 Sendler received the Order of the White Eagle. In 2006, the Children of the Holocaust association and the American "Life in a Jar" foundation, with the Polish foreign ministry's support, established the Irena Sendler Award "For Healing the World." In 2007, Irena Sendler was nominated for the Nobel Peace Prize. ◄►

Chapter 12 - She Hid Jews in a German Officer's Mansion

By: Curtis M. Urness, Sr.

Irene Gut-Opdyke was a teenager when the Nazi attack on Poland changed her life forever. She was separated from her family, escaped twice from incarceration, and captured and raped by Soviet soldiers. Her most difficult predicament was also her noblest: she saved the lives of 16 Polish Jews, hiding some of them literally beneath the noses of the German officers.

The actions of rescuers during the Holocaust not only placed them into danger but also forced them to seek help from unlikely sources. Young Irene Gut had not planned to become a heroine. She found herself in a situation in which she could help and utilized that situation. To say that her behavior was atypical of the Polish community is a generalization that overlooks the complex situation that existed in occupied Poland.

Irene's activities as a rescuer began ironically with her own capture by the Germans to serve as a slave laborer. She had just returned to Radom, in Nazi-occupied Poland, from Ternopol, under Soviet occupation, where her ill treatment by the Soviet military had occurred. She was arrested one day while at church in a lapanka, a roundup of Polish citizens. German soldiers actually interrupted Mass and herded the parishioners into the streets. Irene was selected for labor and loaded in a truck with other prisoners. She was sent to work in a munitions factory, where she fell ill.

A German officer, Major Eduard Rugemer, felt pity for her and gave her a position in the kitchen of a hotel for Nazis.

It was at the hotel, which was located next to the Glinice ghetto in Radom, that Irene observed firsthand the treatment of the Jews by the Nazis. One day, while setting tables, she heard gunfire. Looking through a window to observe what was happening, she saw soldiers shooting the unarmed ghetto inhabitants and turning attack dogs on them. Just as she was about to scream, Schulz, the German chef, held his hand over her mouth. "Don't cry--they will think you are a Jew-lover," he warned. It was after this terrible mass murder that Irene began helping Jews. She would put leftovers in box and leave them just inside the ghetto fence. She did this despite proclamations that anyone caught aiding a Jew would be put to death.

In April of 1942, Major Rugemer's unit was moved to Lwów. The month before the move the Glinice ghetto was liquidated and bulldozed under. Radom had been proclaimed "Jew-free." In Lwów, two things happened that set Irene closer to her course as a rescuer. There she befriended Helen Weinbaum; a Polish Catholic married to a Jewish man. Helen's husband, Henry, was an inmate at a nearby Arbeitslager, a work camp. After receiving word that the SS was holding all Jews from the Arbeitslagers and the neighboring ghettoes in village, Irene, Helen, and Irene's sister, Janina, went to the village to find Henry. There they discovered the SS rushing the Jews out of houses and shooting those whom did not run fast enough. Elderly Jews and women with children were their principle targets. Undoubtedly, the most gruesome act that Irene witnessed was a German officer tossing an infant into the air like a clay pigeon and shooting the child. He then shot the grieving mother. The surviving prisoners were then marched out of the village.

In another ironic twist, the major's unit was sent to Ternopol, scene of Irene's trials with Soviets. There Major Rugemer was commander of a factory, called Harres-Krafa-Park (HKP). Irene resumed her work in the dining hall and kitchen. In the course of her duties, Irene met Jewish workers in the hotel laundry room. She began helping them by giving them extra food and blankets, and recommending them for work in the kitchen. Schulz, the chef, helped her provide these items, although he did not acknowledge what he was doing. Unfortunately, some of the Jews began to disappear. Irene's friend, Fanka Silberman, heard her family being taken away as she hid. Two kitchen helpers, Roman and Sozia, were sent away after being betrayed by a local girlfriend of the SS chief, Rokita. Irene overheard rumors of another raid from Germans eating in the dining hall. It was after these occurrences that Irene became an active smuggler and rescuer.

Irene drove six of the Jews, including Henry Weinbaum, who had not been killed in the raid and now had the dubious job of valet for Rokita, in a dorozka, a wagon, to the forest of Puszcza Janowska. Once safe in the forest, her contraband passengers escaped into its dark reaches. In the nearby town, Irene met a sympathetic Polish Catholic priest, Father Joseph. Later she met a Polish forester, Zygmunt Pasiewski, a former partisan, who would help her care for two of the Jewish ladies, one of whom, Ida Haller, would have a baby at his cottage.

The most ironic twist was yet to come. As the liquidation of the ghetto drew near, Irene determined to save her remaining Jewish friends. They hid behind a false wall in the HKP laundry room on the night of the raid. The next night she led to their next hiding place -- a heating duct inside Major Rugemer's apartment.

The ironies did not end there. Major Rugemer decided that he would live in a villa in town. He requisitioned the former home of a Jewish architect and appointed Irene to oversee the work. The villa turned out to be the perfect hiding place. Servants' quarters were located in the basement and a bunker was accessible beneath the yard. What transpired afterward could have been the plot of a commedia d'el arte. A Nazi German officer -- a doddering old man--lived at ease without knowing that Jews were hidden beneath his feet. At one point, Irene had to interrupt the visiting Rokita, who was in-flagrante with a woman at the gazebo directly above the bunker.

Finally she was found out by Major Rugemer. He came home one afternoon and discovered Fanka Silberman and Ida Bauer upstairs with Irene. He was angry but he was also trapped: it would not look good for a Nazi officer to have had Jews hiding in his own house. So Major Rugemer became an unlikely rescuer. However, he did demand a price for his silence. Irene was forced to become his mistress.

When the advancing Soviet troops approached Ternopol, Irene was able to take her charges into the forest where they would be liberated. Through the efforts of one young Polish woman, who found herself in an unusual situation, Fanka Silberman, Henry Weinbaum, Moses Steiner,

Marian Wilner, Joseph Weiss, Alex Rosen, David Rosen, Lazar Haller, Clara Bauer, Thomas Bauer, Abram Klinger, Miriam Morris, Hermann Morris, Herschel Morris, and Pola Morris were saved from the Nazi death camps. ◄►

Chapter 13 - Fake Epidemic Saves a Village

By: Ryan Bank

In a time when innocent people were brutally murdered only for their nationality and religion, one soldier stands out among the rest. He defied the Germans, repeatedly risking his life to save the lives of thousands. Dr. Eugene Lazowski is considered a hero to many, but for him, saving others was his only option it was simply the right thing to do.

Dr. Lazowski was a soldier and doctor in the Polish Army, Polish Underground Army and Red Cross during World War II. Based on a medical discovery by his friend, Stanislaw Matulewicz, he created a fake epidemic of a dangerous infectious disease, Epidemic Typhus, in the town Rozwadow, as well as surrounding villages.

Injection of Bacteria Saves Lives

The doctors discovered if they injected a healthy person with a "vaccine" of killed bacteria, that person would test positive to Epidemic Typhus. In secrecy, Dr. Matulewicz tested it on a friend who was on special leave from a work camp in Germany. He desperately needed a way to avoid going back to face death in the work camp and becoming just another number. He injected the man with the bacteria and sent a blood sample to the German laboratory. About a week later, the young doctors received a telegraph informing them their patient had Epidemic Typhus, which prohibited the man's return to the work camp. It worked.

He repeated this process on anyone who was sick, creating an epidemic. The Germans were terrified of the disease, not to mention very susceptible to it--they hadn't been infected with it in many years. With each case of Typhus, the Germans would send a red telegram a few more lives were saved. When the disease reached epidemic proportions, the Germans quarantined the area. No additional people were sent to concentration or work camps. Also, no Germans entered the area.

It looked promising for the young doctor until the Germans sent a medical inspection team into the region to verify the disease. The team comprised of a few doctors and several armed soldiers, met Dr. Lazowski just outside the city, where a hot meal awaited the team. They started eating and drinking with the young doctor. The lead doctor was having fun drinking, and thereby sent the younger two doctors to the hospital. Fearing for their own safety, they only drew blood samples and left. Dr. Lazowski knew he had succeeded.

He saved 8,000 people from certain death in Nazi concentration camps. It was his private war of intellect, not weapons. Dr. Lazowski followed in his parents footsteps, which helped save the lives of Jewish people during the holocaust. His parents, later named Righteous Gentiles, hid two Jewish families in their home. While Dr. Lazowski didn't hide families, he did help many Jews medically against German orders.

Medical Help for Jews in the Ghetto

He lived next to a Jewish ghetto in Rozwadow; his back fence bordered the neighborhood. The Jews needed medical attention, so he arranged a system with them. Since it was punishable by death to help any Jewish person, he had to be secretive. If any Jews needed his help, they were to hang a white piece of cloth on his back fence, where he would help them in the safety of the night. Every night the white cloth would fly; lines formed waiting for his help they trusted him. He aided anyone who needed help, creating a system of faking his medicinal inventory to conceal his help of Jews.

Dr. Lazowski also faced death several other times in the war. He was working on a Polish Red Cross train, caring for injured soldiers. With the train stopped, he left to find food for the wounded, only to return to total chaos the Germans used the red crosses as bombing targets. The injured on their way home would never see their families again.

Dr. Lazowski also spent time in a prisoner-of-war camp prior to his arrival in Rozwadow. Determined to find a way out, he started to size up the security. A 3 meter wall with barbed wire surrounded the camp. He noticed a break in the barbed wire and took off. With a thief's leap, whereby he took a running start and two steps on the face of the wall, he was over. Sure the guard heard him, he ran to a nearby horse and cart, whose driver was missing. Dr. Lazowski started to pet the horse and adjust the bridle, as if it were his own animal. The guard looked over and Dr. Lazowski simply smiled and said a kind word to him. The guard thought nothing of it, and Dr. Lazowski was off to safety.

Towards the end of the war, Dr. Lazowski left Rozwadow when a German soldier, whom he had helped several months earlier, warned him that the Germans were going to kill him. They were on to his scheme. His wife and young daughter at his side, Dr. Lazowski ran out through their back fence for Warsaw. As he looked down the street, he saw that same soldier killing Jewish children. It sent chills down his spine. Dr. Lazowski left the town he personally saved forever. ◄►

Chapter 14 - Dutch Doctor and Member of the Underground

Julda was a girl of 12 in Amsterdam and when she witnessed one of her father's courageous actions to save the Jewish family living in the apartment above theirs. When the Gestapo came to take the family to a concentration camp, her father lied, saying that one of the boys had scarlet fever and was quarantined for six weeks. As a member of the Dutch underground, Zubli later arranged for the family members to hide on a Dutch farm.

A medal and certificate were posthumously awarded recently to Dr. Julius Zubli, a Dutch physician who's heroic and humanitarian actions saved several Jews during the Holocaust of World War II.

Zubli himself was later sent to a German concentration camp for giving medical aid to an underground leader. However, it was the quick reaction of her mother that saved her father s life immediately after his arrest, Julda said.

"I remember that day so well," she said. Her mother dressed up beautifully to impress the German police and hurried to police headquarters to retrieve the patient notebook her husband always carried with him.

The Gestapo suspiciously checked the book a number of times, reluctant to give it back to her. She insisted the book was needed by the replacement doctor to continue treatments for Dr. Zubli s patients.

"It was a good thing she got it back," said Rudolph Joon. The book contained code names of people in the Dutch

Underground, plus details of escape routes throughout Europe.

"If the Gestapo had learned that, he would have been killed," Joon said.

Although he wasn't Jewish, Julda said her father was a "humanist" who would have helped anyone. The Joon family has donated the doctor s concentration camp striped uniform and identification bracelet to the U.S. Holocaust Museum. ◄►

Chapter 15 - The Legacy for the Next Generation

When my mother became gravely ill several years ago, my mind filled with weighty thoughts. In addition to feeling frightened about being orphaned again, I realized that no matter how old you are, the death of an ultimate parent still represents an end to your childhood. As long as my mother is alive, I am still someone's child. But, once she is gone, I will have to rely on my memories.

I'm glad that I took the time to talk to my mother about her life - especially the life she lead before she gave birth to me and my sister. It amazed me how little I knew about someone I have known all of my life. For the first time, my mother shared her very personal stories about enduring the War -- about working in Germany as a slave laborer.

After listening to the stories of the Holocaust from my mother and other survivors, I realize that I have received a weighty bequest -- the legacy of a second generation survivor.

The children of Holocaust survivors have begun to speak out about how their lives have been impacted being born to survivors. As the second generation survivors pass through parenthood and middle age, they are showing concern about the legacy they have been handed down by their parents.

This enormous legacy can be a burden or a gift. For those who have accepted this ponderous legacy, I have some words of encouragement: You are not alone. Your feelings are shared by countless others. This is especially important for non-Jewish second generation survivors. The children of non-Jewish survivors have felt much the same pain and burden as children of Jewish survivors -- with one major difference. Non- Jewish children of survivors are often denied the recognition. Many are not aware that they were victims of the Holocaust too -- some just as much or almost just as much as many of their Jewish friends.

Because the Jewish people have worked diligently to make sure that their children do not forget the tragedies of the Holocaust, non-Jewish survivors have often felt that, by comparison, their parents did not suffer "enough" and that the Holocaust is a "Jewish thing". There is no doubt that the Jewish people as a whole suffered much more than the non-Jews. Whether one group suffered more is not an issue. There is no yardstick for personal suffering. Personal misery and sorrow cannot be measured. Nor should it be denied.

Non-Jewish children often do not have the same extensive support groups and backup organizations as Jewish children of survivors. There are many support groups and organizations for second generation survivors, but, from my experience, these groups are almost exclusively Jewish. So, non-Jewish children of survivors are again being forgotten -- just like their parents.

To some second generation children, it does not matter. Some feel no burden of being children of survivors. Some feel no desire to accept the legacy as a gift. This bequest is not for everyone. But, for those who accept the legacy of the Holocaust as a gift, I urge you to exploit this precious bequest. It is a part of your history too.

Do not let anyone deny that your parents, your grandparents or your family suffered. Remember that your parents and grandparents were also incarcerated, tortured, enslaved and murdered. Remember that your parents and grandparents fought valiantly with crude homemade weapons, tools and utensils. Remember this important part of your history, not only to honor your forefathers, but also for your children's sake. One day it will be your turn to pass the legacy on to them. ◄►

Terese Pencak Schwartz

Bibliography

Friedman, Ina R. *The Other Victims - First-Person Stories of Non-Jews Persecuted by the Nazis*. Boston: Houghton Mifflin Company, 1990

Korbonski, Stefan. *Jews and the Poles in World War II*. U.S.A.: Hippocrene Books, 1989

Lukas, Richard C. *Forgotten Holocaust: The Poles Under German Occupation, 1939-1944*. U.S.A.: Hippocrene Books, 1990.

Tomaszewski, Irene. *Zegota: The rescue of Jews in Wartime Poland*. U.S.A.: Price-Patterson, 1994

Wood, Thomas E. and Jankowski, Stanislaw. *KARSKI: How One Man Tried to Stop the Holocaust*. U.S.A. John Wiley & Sons, Inc., 1996